# Harry Houdini
## Escape Artist

written by
**Patricia Lakin**

illustrated by
**Rick Geary**

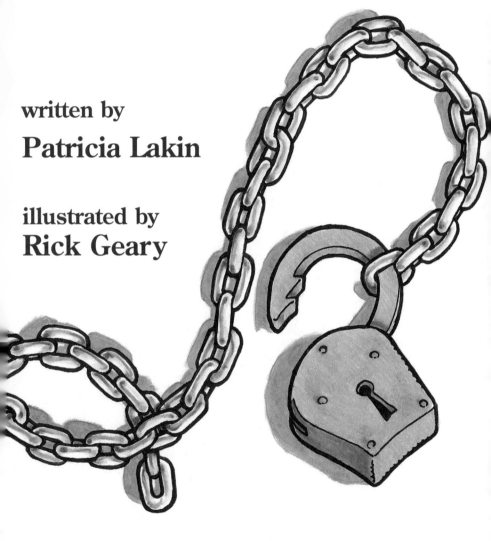

Aladdin

**New York** **London** **Toronto** **Sydney** **Singapore**

**For Steve Geck who offered encouragement, and for Steve Fraser who offered praise and opportunities.**
**—P. L.**
**For Deborah.**
**—R. G.**

First Aladdin Paperbacks edition September 2002

Text copyright © 2002 by Patricia Lakin

Illustrations copyright © 2002 by Rick Geary


ALADDIN PAPERBACKS

An imprint of Simon & Schuster Children's Publishing Division

1230 Avenue of the Americas

New York, NY 10020

Book design by Lisa Vega

The text of this book was set in Century Old Style.


Printed in the United States of America

6 8 10 9 7

0212 LAK

Library of Congress Cataloging-in-Publication Data

Lakin, Pat.

Harry Houdini and the shiny coins / written by Patricia Lakin.—1st Aladdin Paperbacks ed.

p. cm. – (Ready-to-read)

Summary: Simple text describes how Harry Houdini, born Ehrich Weiss, worked hard to become a great magician.

ISBN 978-0-689-85345-6 (Aladdin Library Edition)

ISBN 978-0-689-84815-5 (Aladdin pbk.)

1. Houdini, Harry, 1874-1926—Juvenile literature. 2. Magicians—United States—Biography—Juvenile literature. 3. Escape artists—United States—Biography—Juvenile literature.

[1. Houdini, Harry, 1874-1926. 2. Magicians.] I. Title. II. Series.

GV1545.H8 L33 2002

793.8'092—dc21

[B]

2001046043

Magician!

Escape artist!

Super-human stunt man!

Who was that and more?

Harry Houdini!

Houdini's real name
was Ehrich Weiss.
He was born in Hungary.
When he was very young,
the family came to America.

4

They settled in Wisconsin.

The family was very poor,

and could not always pay the rent.

So they moved many times.

Finally, they came to New York.

Instead of going to school,

Ehrich and his younger brother

Theo had to work.

But working had its bright si
Theo's boss showed him
how to make a coin disappear
Theo showed the trick
to thirteen-year-old Ehrich.

Ehrich was fascinated!

He did the trick very well.

Ehrich had what magicians need—

quick, strong hands.

9

From then on, Ehrich spent his
free time learning new tricks.
He knew that to be
a really good magician
he had to be smart, strong,
and sure of himself.

Being sure of himself
helped at work too.

One December, Ehrich had a job
as a department-store messenger.

He pinned a sign onto his uniform.

It said, "Christmas is coming.

Turkeys are fat.

Please put a quarter

in the Messenger Boy's hat."

13

Ehrich hid the quarters
in his thick hair,
up his sleeves,
and up his pant legs.

Ehrich told his mother,
"Shake me. I'm magic."
Shiny silver quarters
spun from his body
and danced on the floor!
Mother and son laughed for joy
as they scooped up the rent money.

Year after year,

Ehrich worked at many jobs.

And year after year,

his passion for magic grew.

Ehrich trained every part of his body.

He needed both hands to be strong.

So he spent hours

tying and untying knots.

His lungs had to be strong too.

So he practiced holding his breath

in the bathtub.

He also trained his mind.

He took apart locks and learned

how they worked.

His favorite library book was by
the world-famous French magician,
Jean Eugène Robert-Houdin.
Ehrich added an "i"
to the end of his idol's last name.
Ehrich's nickname, "Ehrie,"
sounded like Harry.
From then on seventeen-year-old
Ehrich Weiss was known
as Harry Houdini.

After years of struggling,
Houdini was finally famous.
In 1912, a New York theater owner
paid him one thousand dollars a week
for his act!
Houdini asked for his salary in coins.

At home, he slowly
spilled the glittering
gold coins onto his mother's lap.
Houdini said that this
was his proudest moment.

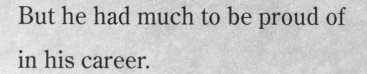

But he had much to be proud of
in his career.
People packed theaters
to see his act.
They filled the streets
to see his stunts.

*Click!*

Houdini was handcuffed.

*Clank!*

He was tied up with locked chains
and put into a box.

*Bam!*

The box was nailed shut.

*Splash!*

The box was thrown into the river!

Crowds watched and waited,
sometimes for hours!
Would he escape alive?
He always did,
and without any help!
But how?

Houdini never told his secrets.

And he never stopped

using his head,

his hands,

and his heart.

### Houdini became the greatest magician the world has ever known.

### Here is a timeline of Harry Houdini's life:

| | |
|---|---|
| 1874 | Born as Ehrich Weiss in Budapest, Hungary |
| 1876 | Ehrich's younger brother, Theo, is born |
| 1878 | Weiss family settles in Appleton, Wisconsin |
| 1887 | Weiss family moves to New York |
| 1891 | Changes his name to Harry Houdini and becomes a full-time magician |
| 1892 | Father dies |
| 1893 | Meets and marries Beatrice (Bess) Rahner. She becomes his partner in the act. |
| 1895 | Uses handcuffs for the first time in his act |
| 1899 | Receives star billing from a famous theater owner, an becomes a big hit all over the world |
| 1907 | Jumps into San Francisco Bay, handcuffed, with a 75-pound ball and chained to his ankles |
| 1908 | Creates the Milk Can Escape, where he escapes from a locked milk can filled with water |
| 1912 | Performs his famous Chinese Water Torture Cell, where he is chained and lowered, head-first, into a glass fronted box filled with water |
| 1912 | Performs at the Hammerstein Theatre in New York at a record salary of $1000 per week |
| 1913 | Mother dies |
| 1913 | Performs for former President Teddy Roosevelt |
| 1915 | Performs for President Woodrow Wilson |
| 1919 | Goes to Hollywood to produce, star, and do stunts for the movies. |
| 1926 | Dies on October 31 |